SEASONS OF LIFE

THE DEVOTIONAL

A. Margot Blair

Printed in The United Stands of America

DEDICATION

To the women who are believing God for a spiritual breakthrough in their lives. You know you were born to make an impact in the lives of others. However, you have been 1) believing false narratives about yourself, 2) practicing habits that no longer serve you in the season you are in or the season God is inviting you into, and 3) hesitating on making disciplined decisions which will allow you surrender to God's will for your life.

I'm here to show (or remind) you that we have a blueprint found through Scripture and an example of the character, attitude, and behaviors which allow us to live our lives more like Christ Jesus. As long as you are willing to allow God to lead, you can always find your way through even the most challenges seasons of life.

IT IS TIME to begin consulting with The One who gave you your vision in the first. **IT IS TIME** to prioritize your faith in your personal (and professional) life. **IT IS TIME** to learn how to navigate through seasons of your life using biblical principles.

Let's dive in.

A. Margot Blair
& The AMB Team

Faith complete
trust or confidence in someor

≫ Table of Contents

PHASE
ONE

FIND FREEDOM IN CHRIST

FIND FREEDOM IN CHRIST: A SEASON OF DARKNESS

"Come to Me, all who are weary and heavily burdened [by religious rituals that provide no peace], and I will give you rest [refreshing your souls with salvation]. Take My yoke upon you and learn from Me [following Me as My disciple], for I am gentle and humble in heart, and you will find rest (renewal, blessed quiet) for your souls."

Matthew 11:28-29 AMP

SEASONS OF LIFE
THE DEVOTIONAL

FIND FREEDOM IN CHRIST: A SEASON OF DARKNESS

Have you ever faced a battle you believed would consume you?

Although, I'm glad I'm not the only one. How do we trust God while we wait for his perfect timing?

Over the last month, I've spoken with several women who were in a challenging season of their life. What troubled me was that they were suffering in silence. I reminded them that the enemy fights for territory. Control is what he wants. The enemy's mission is to steal, kill, and destroy (John 10:10). We must also acknowledge Jesus' reminder that we "have the authority over all the power of the enemy" (Luke 10:19).

There are two choices to make when we experience the fiery darts of the enemy. 1) To believe the truth he has twisted into a lie, or 2) to respond the way Christ did in Matthew 4 when the enemy tried to tempt Jesus.

Instead of accepting defeat, Christ stood firm in his Kingdom Identity. This demonstration shows how we should respond when the enemy tries to tempt us, steal from us, kill us, or destroy us (John 10:10). While we press into God during seasons of warfare and ambiguity, we will eventually come out on the other side with a powerful testimony. You just have to wait (and not worry) while God leads you through the "eventually." He's got you covered.

FIND FREEDOM IN CHRIST: A SEASON OF DARKNESS

PRAYER

Lord, I repent. For far too long, I have been holding on to beliefs that don't serve me in the season you have me in, or the season you are inviting me into. Not only am I on the opposite side of my dreams, but I also am not living the life you have for me. Today, I ask for your guidance as I surrender my burdens to you. I want to live a life that honors you. In Jesus' name, Amen.

READING FOR THIS SEASON

- Matthew 11:28-29 AMP
- Ephesians 6:12
- Hebrews 13:5 NIV
- Exodus 4:14
- Psalm 62:1-2
- James 4:7-8 The Message

YOUR REFLECTIONS

FIND FREEDOM IN CHRIST:
A SEASON OF DARKNESS

FIND FREEDOM IN CHRIST: A SEASON OF GENESIS

"Now may the God of peace Himself sanctify you through and through [that is, separate you from profane and vulgar things, make you pure and whole and undamaged—consecrated to Him—set apart for His purpose]; and may your spirit and soul and body be kept complete and [be found] blameless at the coming of our Lord Jesus Christ."

1 Thessalonians 5:23 AMP

SEASONS OF LIFE
THE DEVOTIONAL

FIND FREEDOM IN CHRIST: A SEASON OF GENESIS

Have you ever wondered, "how do I put God FIRST if things in my personal or professional life aren't going the way I believe they should be?"

If so, this message is specifically for you. Foremost, you're not the first one to ask God this question. Second, your willingness to ask this question reveals that you are open to receiving what God has planned for you.

Now, I do not have a "do this, and you'll never doubt or worry again" message for you. Honestly, if someone tries to give you one of those, RUN!

What I have for you today is a recommendation. Take a moment to read Matthew 6:33, and other biblical texts that will offer you insight when you navigate a new or challenging season of your life. As you invite God to do a new thing in your life, he will also develop your attitude and character so that you become more like him. You must understand and be willing to see yourself the way he sees you.

PRAYER

Lord, thank you! Thank you for impressing on my heart a desire to understand your vision for my life. I have more questions than answers in this season of my life. I understand I am a vessel, hand-picked for your good works. Use me, Lord. As I read your word, help me see from your perspective. Be my

FIND FREEDOM IN CHRIST:
A SEASON OF GENESIS

interpreter, so I can fully understand the intended meaning you speak through the living word. Guide me as I put your instructions into practice in my life. Use me to lead your people to seek, learn from, and follow you. In Jesus' name. Amen.

READING FOR THIS SEASON

- 1 Thessalonians 5:23 AMP
- Philippians 3:13-14 AMP
- Matthew 6:33
- Ephesians 1
- Ephesians 2

YOUR REFLECTIONS

FIND FREEDOM IN CHRIST:
A SEASON OF GENESIS

PHASE TWO

BREAK FREE FROM STRONGHOLDS

BREAK FREE FROM STRONGHOLDS:
A SEASON OF CHANGE

"Therefore if you have been raised with Christ [to a new life, sharing in His resurrection from the dead], keep seeking the things that are above, where Christ is, seated at the right hand of God."

COLOSSIANS 3:1 AMP

SEASONS OF LIFE
THE DEVOTIONAL

BREAK FREE FROM STRONGHOLDS: A SEASON OF CHANGE

Change is inevitable. Sometimes, the invitation to change can expose the symptoms of the spirit of fear. Whether you fear failure (not achieving a particular goal) or fear of success (not knowing what is on the other side of your obedience to God), you must do the work to get the root to overcome the fear.

During seasons of change, we must learn to give ourselves grace. If we aren't aware, the environments, people, and other things around us can attempt to woo or convince us back to the old ways of doing things. Years ago, I came across some research that suggested a person cannot get rid of old and unhealthy habits that no longer serve the individual. The study revealed that we can override old, unhealthy habits with new ones (National Institute of Health, 2012).

Navigating through a season of change requires you to take an inventory of your current way of thinking about your response to the change occurring in your life. In Luke 13:5 (AMP), we learn unless we repent [change our old way of thinking, turn from our sinful ways, and live changed lives] we will all likewise perish. Even when your circumstances change, consider what it might cost you if you're unwilling to embrace change.

BREAK FREE FROM STRONGHOLDS:
A SEASON OF CHANGE

ACTION STEP

Write one thing you can do daily to strengthen your commitment to God.

_____

_____

READING FOR THIS SEASON

- Luke 13:5 ERV
- Colossians 3:1–10 AMP
- John 8:31–32 AMP
- Galatians 5:1 NIV

YOUR REFLECTIONS

_____

_____

_____

_____

_____

_____

BREAK FREE FROM STRONGHOLDS:
A SEASON OF CHANGE

BREAK FREE FROM STRONGHOLDS:
A SEASON OF TRANSITION

"So get rid of everything evil in your lives—every kind of wrong you do. Be humble and accept God's teaching that is planted in your hearts. This teaching can save you. Do what God's teaching says; don't just listen and do nothing. When you only sit and listen, you are fooling yourselves."

James 1:21-22 ERV

SEASONS OF LIFE
THE DEVOTIONAL

BREAK FREE FROM STRONGHOLDS:
A SEASON OF TRANSITION

Some people see change and transition interchangeably. If you're one of these people, I invite you to consider an alternative perspective.

Imagine standing in front of a body of water. This body of water can be a pond, lake, or even a swimming pool. Now, look down. Near your feet, you see a pebble or rock that can fit into the palm of your hand. You pick up the pebble or rock. Then, you throw it into the water in front of you. *This is the change.* As the rock enters the water, you see ripples on top of the water. *This is the transition.*

Let's unpack this analogy of navigating more effectively through the seasons of your life. A change occurred when you picked up the rock and threw it into the water. Something was physically different. The ripples you pictured above the water are the transitions. Although you may not know how the change impacted the rock, residue from the old environment may still be attached.

The same is true for us. Rather than focusing on the change that has already happened. Consider what you are feeling or experiencing on the other side of the change. The most important thing you can do during a season of transition is to invite God to be part of your learning process.

BREAK FREE FROM STRONGHOLDS: A SEASON OF TRANSITION

ACTION STEP

Here are three practical steps you can take during a season of transition: 1) notice your habits, 2) know how to respond when unhealthy habits try to resurface, and 3) be intentional as you put the new habits into practice.

READING FOR THIS SEASON

- James 1:21-22 ERV
- Ephesians 4:20-24
- Philippians 4:6
- 2 Corinthians 3:18

YOUR REFLECTIONS

_____

_____

_____

_____

_____

_____

_____

BREAK FREE FROM STRONGHOLDS:
A SEASON OF TRANSITION

PHASE THREE

GROW IN SPIRITUAL MATURITY

GROW IN SPIRITUAL MATURITY:
A SEASON OF RELEASE

"You, therefore, will be perfect [growing into spiritual maturity both in mind and character, actively integrating godly values into your daily life], as your heavenly Father is perfect."

Matthew 5:48 AMP

SEASONS OF LIFE
THE DEVOTIONAL

GROW IN SPIRITUAL MATURITY:
A SEASON OF RELEASE

When you find yourself in a season of release, allow yourself to be set free from any condemnation, comparison, or any other limiting belief that tries to creep in. John 8:32 (TPT-The Passion Translation), reminds us when we embrace the truth, it will release true freedom into our lives.

Today, practice surrendering your cares to God. Learn to develop the habit of believing God's truth in our situations. A way to allow this process to become second nature to you is learning how to R.E.S.T. (Psalm 119 AMP).

R.E.S.T. stands for:

- **R**econnect with your source (God).
- **E**nhance your time in worship.
- **S**urrender to God's will for your life.
- **T**rust the longevity of God's process for you.

Start by positioning yourself in contemplative prayer (Matthew 6:9-13). Then, read the following words aloud before God:

PRAYER

Lord, thank you for the new measure of grace and mercy you extend to me each day. Through Christ, I'm reminded of the freedom I find in you. Over the last several days, you have helped me break free from strongholds that I allowed to define me for far

GROW IN SPIRITUAL MATURITY:
A SEASON OF RELEASE

too long. I ask that you continue to remind me of what it looks like walking Matthew 5:48 out in my life. Your word says, "[I] therefore will be perfect". In the Amplified translation, I understand that perfect means growing in spiritual maturity both in mind and character, actively integrating godly values into my daily life.

Through this refining process, you are teaching me to become more like you, God. Thank you for the work that you were doing with me. Thank you for having gone before me to prepare for the way. God, I pray that you continue to reveal what you need me to see in this season of my life. Also, prepare me to make disciples of others. I thank you, God. I give you all the honor, glory, and praise. In Jesus' mighty and powerful name, Amen.

READING FOR THIS SEASON

- Matthew 5:48 AMP
- Luke 14:27 AMP
- John 8:31-32
- Hebrews 6:1 AMP
- Matthew 11:28-30 MSG

YOUR REFLECTIONS

GROW IN SPIRITUAL MATURITY:
A SEASON OF RELEASE

GROW IN SPIRITUAL MATURITY:
A SEASON OF LONGEVITY

"Keep your eyes straight ahead;
ignore all sideshow distractions.
Watch your step, and the road will
stretch out smooth before you.
Look neither right nor left; leave
evil in the dust."

Proverbs 4:23-27 MSG

SEASONS OF LIFE
THE DEVOTIONAL

GROW IN SPIRITUAL MATURITY: A SEASON OF LONGEVITY

Have you ever received instructions you know were from God, but the path to put the plan into play was unclear? Details were missing. You had the what, but you needed to identify, or better understand, the how. You discovered the how, but it left you wondering when you were supposed to take the first, next step.

Whether God has given you only a few details of the larger vision, or you have been waiting longer than you hoped, the time eventually arrives when God's word always comes to pass.

I encourage you to ask yourself, "What does it look like for me to trust God while I wait for his next instruction?"

Throughout scripture, we learn biblical principles that we can put into practice in our own lives. Three key lessons that help us learn to trust God while we wait, include:

1) Seek God's kingdom and righteousness WITHOUT being anxious about details he hasn't yet provided (Matthew 6:33-34).

2) God's divine power is NOT our own, yet he equips us with what we need when we need it (2 Peter 1:2-15 AMP).

GROW IN SPIRITUAL MATURITY:
A SEASON OF LONGEVITY

3) There is a designated time, or season, for everything (Genesis 8:22; Ecclesiastes 3:1-11).

We must be sensitive to the Holy Spirit, so we're ready to move when God says to move. We must learn to respond in obedience so that we don't exhaust ourselves trying to outpace him. When we obey, we're able to hear, listen, and trust God (Luke 11:14-36) while we wait. In his timing, we discover God is a promise keeper because this is who he is.

PRAYER

Lord, thank you for keeping your promises. I know the importance of being dialed into your frequency so that I can hear you. In this season, you remind me how important it is for me to remain in step with you. I cannot outpace you, so I might as well not even try. You have my best interest in mind and I trust you even when I am unsure where the steps you are ordering me to follow will lead me. I honor you, Amen.

READING FOR THIS SEASON

- Proverbs 4:23-27 MSG
- Philippians 4:11-14
- Deuteronomy 31:8
- John 15:5-8
- 2 Timothy 4:2-5 ESV

YOUR REFLECTIONS

GROW IN SPIRITUAL MATURITY:
A SEASON OF DISTINCTION

"Constantly rejoicing in hope [because of our confidence in Christ], steadfast and patient in distress, devoted to prayer [continually seeking wisdom, guidance, and strength]..."

Romans 12:12 AMP

SEASONS OF LIFE
THE DEVOTIONAL

GROW IN SPIRITUAL MATURITY:
A SEASON OF DISTINCTION

Are you willing to use what God has placed in your hands?

Instead of waiting for the perfect time, more resources, or an opportunity that seems just right, it will serve you to take the first next step that God has already instructed you to take. In Matthew 25:14-30, we learn the importance of not burying our talents, or in that parable, not burying our money. Also, 2 Peter 1:2-15, remind us that we already have everything we need from God.

If you are watching God's call coming in, but haven't answered. Then, you will want to pay close attention to this message on navigating through a season of distinction.

It's a combination of tough love and practical accountability. God has given you authority. He has also revealed parts of his plan for you. So why are you stalling on taking action? What beliefs are you believing about yourself that God has reminded you repeatedly are NOT true?

Be bold as you find freedom in Christ - yes, even the mature followers. Break free from strongholds that are keeping you from taking your first next step, and grow in spiritual maturity (there's always more for us to learn).

ACTION STEP

As you reflect on each season we discussed in this devotional, ask God to show you what blockers you need to dismantle, so you can use what he has already given you. Then, do one thing daily where you surrender to God, listen more attentively and take strategic action toward the vision he continues to reveal to you.

Remember that God has prepared a special place for you.

READING FOR THIS SEASON

- Romans 12:2 AMP
- 2 Thessalonians 2:13–17
- 1 Chronicles 28:9
- Ephesians 5:1–2
- Joshua 1:9
- Act 1:8

YOUR REFLECTIONS

DAY 07 — GROW IN SPIRITUAL MATURITY: A SEASON OF DISTINCTION

MEET THE MENTOR

Hey There!

I'm so excited you are here! If you're new to me, Hey there. I am A. Margot Blair. I'm a International Christian Author, educator, and personal development consultant. I develop women at the intersection of faith and business.

As a **seasoned and certified personal and leadership development consultant**, I have studied the psychology behind personal and organizational leadership development for over a decade.

Today, I have the incredible honor of equipping and working with organizations, business leaders, and women from around the globe with **adaptive leadership, designing partnership campaigns, client retention strategies, authority/thought leaderships, and biblical personal development**.

As well, our e-Learning resources, live events, and private client experiences have **cultivated the space for more than 11,000 women to learn, heal, and grow** in their personal and professional lives.

A. Margot Blair

PERSONAL & LEADERSHIP DEVELOPMENT CONSULTANT

"Our life experiences do not have to define us. Instead, we can acknowledge them, learn from them, and allow them to serve as stepping stones as we become the women God has predestined us to be."
-A. Margot Blair

WWW.AMARGOTBLAIR.COM

Are you Familiar with a *Faith-Informed Approach* to Personal Development?

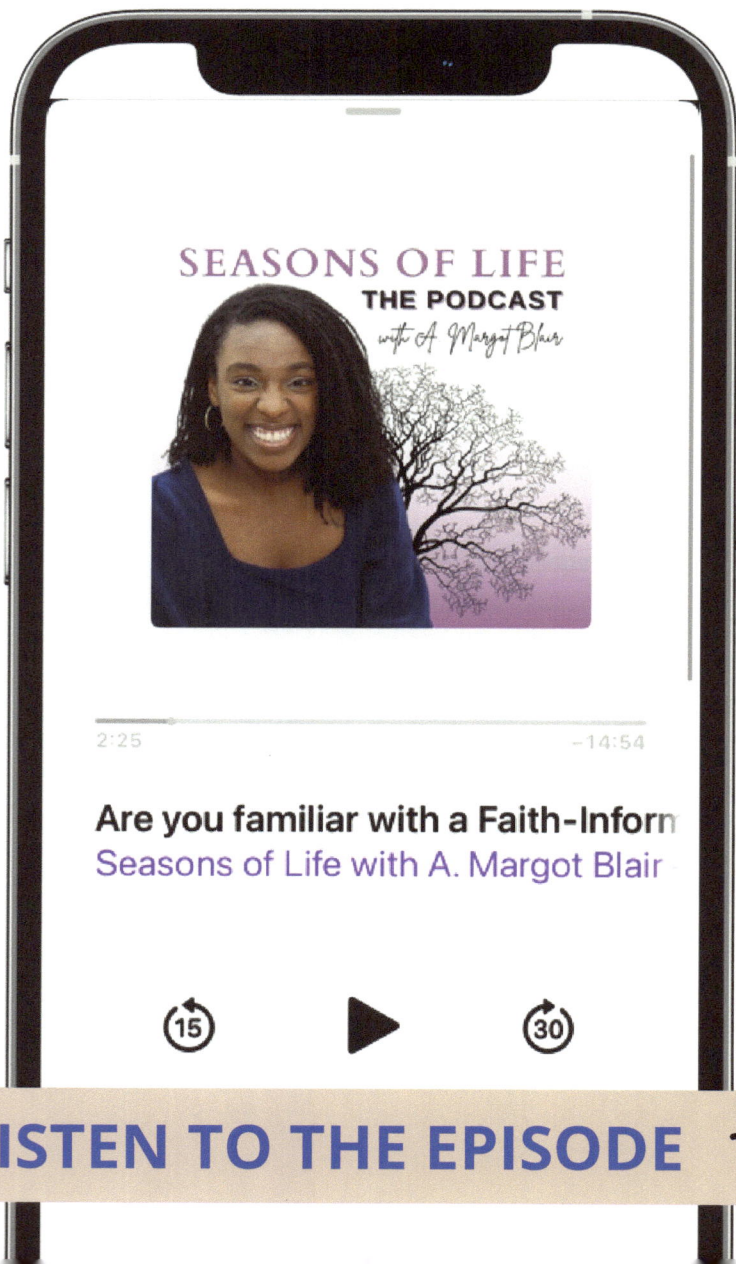

SEASONS OF LIFE
THE PODCAST
with A. Margot Blair

2:25   −14:54

Are you familiar with a Faith-Inforn
Seasons of Life with A. Margot Blair

LISTEN TO THE EPISODE

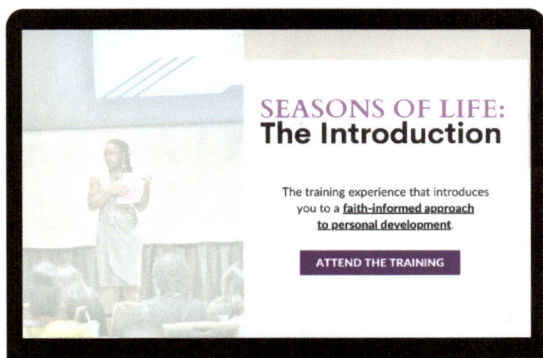

Seasons of Life:
The Introduction

Seasons of Life: The Introduction is a 90-minute, training introducing you to a biblical approach to personal development.

There are Four Central Learning Objectives within this training:

1. Learn a bible-based approach to self-care
2. Discover the season of your life God has you in
3. Identify and understand the root of what is interfering or keeping you from the life God has predestined for you
4.. See your life experiences from God's vantage point

ATTEND TRAINING

REGISTER NOW: WWW.AMARGOTBLAIR.COM

Seasons of Life:
The Community

A community where you learn a practical and biblically based approach to personal development.

Gain access to **Seasons of Life: The Community**, a community designed to teach, equip, and lead women to navigate through the seasons of your life using biblical principles.

WHAT'S INSIDE THE COMMUNITY:

- Seven (7) week Seasons of Life (curricula)
- Digital workbooks
- Interactive activities and exercises for each module
- Monthly gatherings

WWW.AMARGOTBLAIR.COM/SEASONSOFLIFE

SEASONS OF LIFE *Live*
The Introduction

PERSONAL DEVELOPMENT TRAINING FOR WOMEN
AT THE INTERSECTION OF FAITH & BUSINESS

Planning your next women's event, conference, personal development training, or DE&I/ERG workshop? Looking for a dynamic speaker who gets your audience dancing, crying, and into action?

A. Margot Blair, author, educator, and personal development consultant, **is known for developing women at the intersection of faith and business**. Over the last decade, she has been committed to **teaching and equipping women in the marketplace, ministry, corporate, and at home** in the areas of identity restoration, personal and professional development, and spiritual growth.

A. Margot Blair's interactive teaching style cultivates a transformative learning experience where challenges are met with practical action steps that fosters collaborative growth and enhances productivity.

A. Margot is excited to partner with you and your ministry. Learn more about inviting A. Margot Blair to speak or hosting a live **Seasons of Life: The Introduction** experience, today at www.amargotblair/keynote.